DATE DUE

PRINTED IN U.S.A.

Yellow Umbrella Books are published by Red Brick Learning
7825 Telegraph Road, Bloomington, Minnesota 55438
http://www.redbricklearning.com

Library of Congress Cataloging-in-Publication Data
Shepard, Daniel
    [Numbers all around. Spanish & English]
    Numbers all around/by Daniel Shepard = Números en todas partes/
por Daniel Shepard.
        p. cm.
    Summary: "Simple text and photos introduce the concept that numbers are
everywhere"—Provided by publisher.
    Includes index.
    ISBN-13: 978-0-7368-6018-5 (hardcover)
    ISBN-10: 0-7368-6018-5 (hardcover)
    1. Number concept—Juvenile literature. I. Title: Números en todas partes. II. Title.
QA141.3.S5418 2006
513—dc22   2005025849

Written by Daniel Shepard
Developed by Raindrop Publishing

Editorial Director: Mary Lindeen
Editor: Jennifer VanVoorst
Photo Researcher: Wanda Winch
Adapted Translations: Gloria Ramos
Spanish Language Consultants: Jesús Cervantes, Anita Constantino
Conversion Assistants: Jenny Marks, Laura Manthe

Photo Credits
Cover: PhotoLink/PhotoDisc; Title Page: Grantpix/Index Stock; Page 4: Gary
Sundermeyer/Capstone Press; Page 6: AFP/Corbis; Page 8: Carl and Ann Purcell/Corbis;
Page 10: S. Meltzer/PhotoLink/PhotoDisc; Page 12: Gary Sundermeyer/Capstone Press;
Page 14: Steve Allen/Brand X Pictures; Page 16: DigitalVision

1 2 3 4 5 6 11 10 09 08 07 06

Numbers All Around

by Daniel Shepard

Números en todas partes

por Daniel Shepard

Yellow Umbrella Books

for early readers

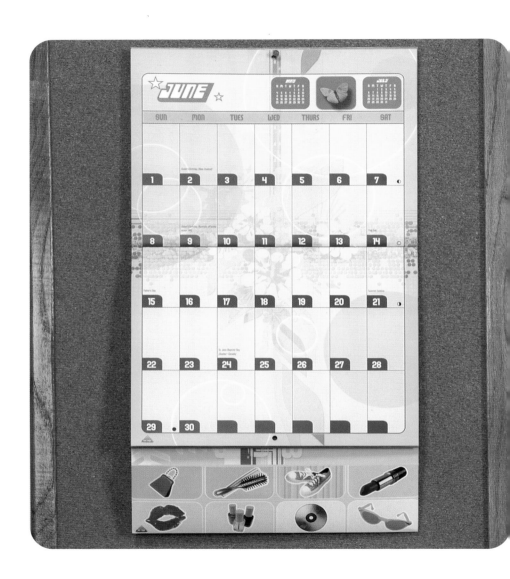

4

I see numbers on the wall.

Veo números en la pared.

I see numbers on
the clock.

Veo números en
el reloj.

8

I see numbers in
the store.

Veo números en
la ventana.

I see numbers on
the team.

Veo números en
las camisetas.

I see numbers on
the house.

Veo números en
la casa.

I see numbers on
the truck.

Veo números en
el camión.

16

Numbers are all
around!

Veo números en
todas partes.

Index

Índice